The Lan

Tra

C000282848

A series of short walks which link
together to form a 70 mile long
distance trail through Lancashire

Connecting
WIDNES, WARRINGTON, ST. HELENS, WIGAN
BOLTON, BLACKBURN & BURNLEY

With

THE PENNINE WAY
at
THORNTON – IN – CRAVEN
and
THE SANDSTONE TRAIL
in
CHESHIRE

BRIAN SMAILES

You will never walk alone with these books published by
Challenge Publications

Top Ten series

THE YORKSHIRE DALES TOP TEN
ISBN 0-9526900-5-5

THE LAKELAND TOP TEN
ISBN 0-9526900-3-9

THE DERBYSHIRE TOP TEN
ISBN 1-903568-03-X

Other books

THE SCOTTISH COAST TO COAST WALK
ISBN 0-9526900-8-X

THE GREAT GLEN WAY
ISBN 1-903568-13-7

17 WALKS IN GLEN NEVIS
ISBN 1-903568-05-6

THE COMPLETE ISLE OF WIGHT COASTAL FOOTPATH
ISBN 0-9526900-6-3

ISLE OF WIGHT, NORTH TO SOUTH – EAST TO WEST
ISBN1-903568-07-2

JOHN O'GROATS TO LANDS END
ISBN 0-9526900-4-7

THE NATIONAL 3 PEAKS WALK
ISBN 0-9526900-7-1

THE YORKSHIRE 3 PEAKS WALK
ISBN 1-903568-01-3

THE 1066 COUNTRY WALK
ISBN 1-903568-00-5

MILLENNIUM CYCLE RIDES IN 1066 COUNTRY
(EAST SUSSEX)
ISBN 1-903568-04-8

TOURIST GUIDE TO VARADERO, CUBA
ISBN 1-903568-08-0

ISBN 1-903568-10-2
FIRST PUBLISHED 2003
CHALLENGE PUBLICATIONS
7, EARLSMERE DRIVE, ARDSLEY, BARNSLEY. S71 5HH

THE AUTHOR

Brian Smailes

Holds the record for the fastest 4 and 5 continuous crossings of the Lyke Wake Walk over the North York Moors. He completed the 210miles over rough terrain on 5 crossings in June 1995 taking 85hours and 50minutes.

Brian lectures on outdoor pursuit courses and between these travels extensively on walking expeditions and other projects around Great Britain and the Caribbean.

Long distance running and canoeing are other sports he enjoys, completing 25 marathons and canoeing the Caledonian Canal 3 times.

His most ambitious venture involved cycling from Lands End to John O`Groats in August 2001, a journey of over 900miles in 6days 13hours 18minutes. This involved carrying food, clothing and tent, and was completed without any support between both ends.

Apart from The Lancashire Trail, other recent expeditions include The Great Glen Way from Fort William to Inverness and The Isle of Wight, North to South - East to West.

ACKNOWLEDGEMENTS

Originally, this route was researched by members of The St. Helens & District CHA & HF Rambling Club and published by their rambles secretary in 1980. Since this publication, much of the route has changed due to building work, new roads, new footpaths, footpath diversions and the onset of time. Consequently, this new edition has been re-written and the route checked and brought up to date.

My thanks go to Arnold Richmond who originally devised the route and saw it through to fruition in 1980 and who has provided invaluable information and assistance for this new edition.

Thanks also to Trevor Atkinson who was my companion on this expedition and for his help and advice where needed.

Photographs – Arnold Richmond, Trevor Atkinson and Brian Smailes.

This Edition
First Published 2003
ISBN 1-903568-10-2
Challenge Publications, 7, Earlsmere Drive, Barnsley. S71 5HH

FOREWORD

The guide is arranged in such a way as to divide the route into a series of inter-connected walks or sections ranging from 3½ to 10miles in length. Starting from St. Helens on Merseyside and finishing 70miles to the northeast on the Pennine Way, at Thornton-in-Craven, on the Lancashire- Yorkshire border.

Access by public transport to the starting points is indicated, together with the route descriptions and 'viewpoints' or 'points of interest'. Availability of transport from the finishing points however is determined by referring to 'Access for the subsequent section'.

This walk takes you through areas of beautiful countryside with meandering streams and leafy lanes, past canals and through woodland to provide you with some of the best walking you will experience. There are sections through built up areas and suburbs and even these areas have their own stories to tell of their industrial heritage.

To shorten the text, public footpaths and public bridleways mentioned in this book are referred to as P.F. and P.B. respectively. All compass bearings shown in the book are given as magnetic bearings.

There are no camping sites on the route and limited bed and breakfast throughout. I recommend that if you require these facilities it would be advisable to telephone the nearest tourist information centre to obtain a current list. The telephone numbers of these are listed in the appendix.

I hope that walking the route described in this book will prove as interesting and rewarding an experience to you as it has to myself.

CONTENTS

Page

PHOTOGRAPHS 1

CLOTHING & EQUIPMENT 2

PHOTOGRAPHS

Page

CLOTHING & EQUIPMENT

It is essential that you have the appropriate clothing and equipment with you when walking in open country. Although there are some short road sections, boots are recommended as most of the route is across fields and on public footpaths/bridleways. Depending on weather conditions, it can prove wet underfoot.

A waterproof jacket is also essential, and walking trousers of some kind, but not jeans as they can chafe the skin when wet and draw the body heat, so giving you hypothermia. You will find it beneficial to carry a pair of gloves and a hat with you to help keep warm.

On this walk I recommend you take a compass and the relevant maps, which are detailed, near the back of this book. Although the route is descriptive, and hopefully it can be followed easily, it helps if you have the maps, to pick out landmarks and other topographical features that are not included in this book.

A survival bag, torch, whistle and a first aid kit are an essential part of your equipment. Take several pairs of walking socks so you can have a change of footwear. You need a change of clothing so that if you get wet at least you have some dry clothes to change into to stop you getting hypothermia. Pack equipment in a waterproof bag inside your rucksack and do not take more than you need. Remember you have to carry it!

Although there are some shops to buy food and drinks from on route, I recommend that you take some with you as this will provide a constant energy source while walking the undulating route as well as helping to maintain a constant body temperature

Tell someone back at base your intended route so they can monitor your progress in case of accidents, not forgetting to telephone them to update your position regularly.

STAGE 1 – ST. HELENS TO RIVINGTON (28¼miles)

1.1 – St. Helens to Billinge (5miles)

Access: -

    The starting point of the walk is from the Town Hall in the very heart of St. Helens, at G.R.512955 readily accessible by means of frequent bus services from surrounding districts and neighbouring towns. A regular train service between Liverpool and Wigan also serves the town, the station being within a ¼mile from the start of the walk.

Route: -

    Leaving the Town Hall, walk the full length of Birchley St., cross over Standish St. then up a grassy slope at the far side. Walk along an open, grassy area with houses on the left and keep left, following the path by the side of a row of trees. Emerge on College St. with Pilkington glassworks opposite. Turn right for approx. 100yds along College St. and right again at a P. F. sign indicating Merton Bank Road & Town Centre.

    After a short distance, cross the brook which feeds into the old St. Helens Canal and pass under the railway at Gerards Bridge to continue walking along the left bank of the St. Helens Canal. On reaching Merton Bank Road, turn right over the canal bridge then immediately left to follow the track on the right hand bank of the canal. Another P.F. sign points to Park Road stay on the towpath on right side until you come to the A58 at Park Road. Cross this road, and proceed to the left on grass behind the row of cottages opposite, keeping Sankey Brook on the right to Boardmans Lane.

    Passing a rugby ground over to your left, cross Boardmans Lane and continue ahead, looking for a path and sewage works on your right side. Just past the sewage works is a canal basin at G.R.542958. Cross the iron footbridge *(Plate 1)* ahead to walk to the left on the right hand bank of the canal. We now have our first glimpse of Billinge Beacon on the skyline ahead *(Plate 2).*

    On reaching the A58 again near the Ship Inn at Blackbrook, cross road and proceed through a kissing gate opposite and along the valley towards Carr Mill Dam, keeping the canal on the left for a short distance. Eventually the path crosses a small brick footbridge, and continues with a stream on your right to pass under the A580 East Lancashire Road. Continue through a kissing gate then under a railway viaduct, with the water chute from Carr Mill Dam over to your right and take the small path ascending to the lane along the top of the dam to cross a metal bridge over the spillway.

3

1.1 St Helens To Billinge.
5 Miles. Route —.—.—.

Not to Scale

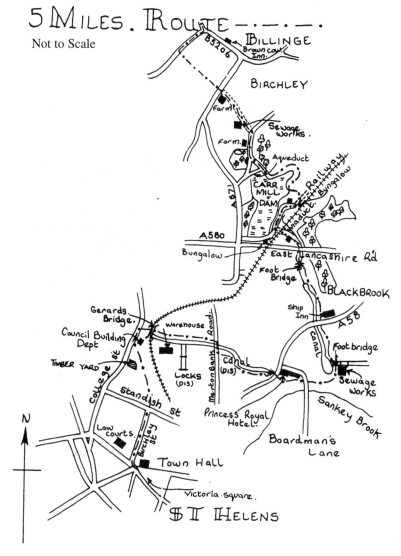

Continue ahead past the Lancs. Powerboat Racing Club building on the left to pass through a kissing gate on the left and follow the path anti-clockwise round the dam keeping to the left all the way to the 19 arch footbridge which carries the St. Helens-Rivington water supply over the dam. At this point continue ahead on a path through trees to join a lane near Otters Swift Farm. Turn right along the lane then go through a narrow opening next to a 5-bar gate in front of the farm. A tower with a weather vane is on the roof.

Take first turning on left past Otters Swift Farm passing sewage works on left to emerge via a farm on Lime Vale Road onto the main road into Billinge. The village centre with its shops and public houses is ½mile up this main road. Continue diagonally right across this road and follow the path opposite along the back of houses and across fields, passing a small pond at the far end onto the B5205 road to Rainford. Turn right, and walk up the road for 650yds to a sharp right hand bend at G.R.522002 at the junction of Red Barn Road.

Points of Interest: -

Since the St. Helens Canal, completed in 1762 was the very first to be constructed, there are naturally several interesting features on the early part of this walk. There are the double locks visible across the canal shortly after Gerard's Bridge, which once provided lift for boats proceeding into the leg of the canal serving the town centre and Ravenhead.

The point where the iron footbridge crosses the canal near the sewage works in St. Helens *(Plate 1)* was once the site of very deep double locks which lowered boats to the floor of the Sankey Valley 60ft below. These have now been filled in for safety reasons with much of the lower part of the canal submerged in the development of the Linear Park, which provides foot access from Earlstown, Newton-le-Willows, Warrington and Widnes (see appendix).

1.2 – Billinge to Abbey Lakes (3½miles)

Access: -

The starting point of this section of the walk is readily accessible from St. Helens or Wigan by means of frequent bus services. One should alight at the Rainford Road junction, at the lower end of the village and proceed along the B5205 Rainford Road to the junction with Red Barn Road.

Route: -

At the above junction G.R.522002 continue along Red Barn Road passing a house and bungalow, to a P. F. on the right at the side of Houghwood House at G.R.521007. Ascend the side of a field towards Billinge Hill, passing a golf course on your left. At a metalled road turn left, walking at the side of that service road towards the beacon. As the road bends right, continue straight ahead, soon to turn right for 60yds, crossing a small field then left towards the tower. On a clear day there are extensive views across Merseyside to the Welsh Hills on the left and also to the Pennine Hills beyond Manchester on the right, as you ascend the hill. Walk to the far side of the beacon, which is 550ft above sea level to see the way ahead and the northern hills.

The track from the summit descends in a N.E. direction to the corner of a fence line where it proceeds north into the wood through a kissing gate. Take a left fork just after entering then within 200yds; turn left onto another path at right angles at G.R.526018, to take you out of the wood via a kissing gate beside a 5-bar gate. Proceed across a field and between a house and old barn onto Crank Road. Cross this road and follow the path ahead, keeping the wire fence on the left to a farm track leading to Brownlow Farm.

Turn left on this track and after 250yds, where the hedge/fence line on the right ends, turn right and continue ahead with the hedgerow on the right, over two stiles. Ahead can be seen Ashurst Beacon with the Trough of Bowland Fells and Winter Hill in the distance to the right, and on a very clear day, the Lake District fells to the left.

On reaching the first lane, which is in a depression, cross this by descending and ascending two short flights of steps at G.R.519024 and continue for 150yds to a second lane by a private residence on the right which has a brick wall at the entrance. At this point, turn left for 50yds; enter the field on the right and head diagonally down the field in a N.W. direction towards Pimbo Bushes, keeping the line of an overgrown wall on your right. On reaching the far end of the field, after 320yds, turn right along a narrow path with the hedgerow on the left, and continue past a stile to a point where the path leads off

6

1.2 Billinge To Abbey Lakes.
3½ Miles. Route ---·---·--

Not to Scale

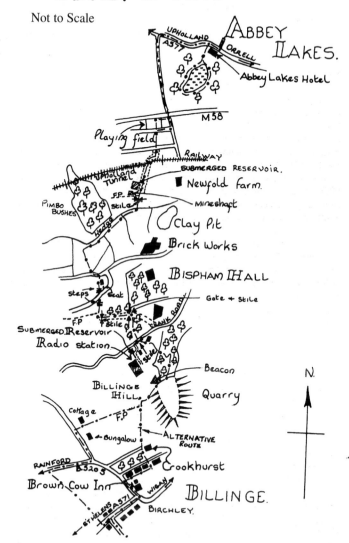

to the left between a wire fence on the left and an overgrown ditch on the right. Follow this track, past a disused mine shaft and an underground reservoir on your left until a playground is reached.

Turning right through the housing estate, and left along Sandbrook road, continue under the M58 motorway bridge along Tontine Road at Upholland. On reaching The White Lion Hotel and St. Thomas Church, turn right to descend School Lane and pass the Owl Inn to reach Abbey Lakes Inn on your right.

Viewpoints: -

On a very clear day the view from Billinge Hill is extensive *(Plate 2),* taking in the Lancashire Fells to the northeast and the central chain of the Pennines to the east. To the south stretches the Cheshire plain and, in the distance to the west, the hills of North Wales.

One can pick out many landmarks in the Manchester and Merseyside areas; these include the Anglican Cathedral of Liverpool and the towering office blocks of central Manchester. In close proximity can be seen the television tower of Winter Hill to the north east and the power station of Fiddlers Ferry to the south, beyond, the glass town of St. Helens.

The original book on this walk guided walkers past Abbey Lakes, a local beauty spot with an abundance of wildlife. Because of the M58 motorway, the walk has been re-routed through Upholland but a visit to Abbey Lakes is recommended if you have time on your walk. Access can be gained by the Abbey Lakes Inn, which is opposite Spencers Road.

1.3 – Abbey Lakes to Parbold Hill (6miles)

Access: -

Frequent bus services from St. Helens, Wigan and Ormskirk provide ready access to the starting point for this section of the walk. One should alight at the Abbey Lakes Inn or if travelling from St. Helens, at the Stag Inn, which is within ½mile.

Route: -

From the Abbey Lakes Inn, cross the road and turn left along Spencers Lane, following a P.F. sign past Dean Wood golf course, where the track veers right then left. On nearing a farm take the path bearing right towards and past a wooded area at the top of a ravine on the left and continue to the end of the hedgerow on the right where there is a crossing path. From here take this path to the left towards woodland, and descend into Dean Wood over a footbridge then over a stream. Turning right, follow the stream; do not ascend the path through the wood.

Stay on the path by the stream, which can be wet and muddy, to a wooden and a metal footbridge. Cross the wooden bridge only then bear left to climb steps out of the ravine into a field. Turn left out of the wood onto a narrow path for 100yds to join an old lane at G.R.529067. Follow a P. F. sign for 1450yds, along this lane to the right, bearing left by trees on a track leading to Walthew Green and Roby Mill.

Emerging in Roby Mill from School Lane, beside the Fox Inn and opposite a row of cottages, turn right, cross the road then turn left behind the last cottage, to follow the P.F. sign on a lamppost. Cross a stile behind the cottage onto a grass path leading across a golf course, keeping to the left of the hedge immediately ahead as you ascend the hillside. At the end of the hedgerow on the right, bear slightly right through the trees to the edge of a short piece of the course and proceed diagonally across the green towards a P.F. sign to emerge onto a minor road.

Turn left up this road for 200yds to a point where the road bears left and follow the P.F. sign along the track to the right for 180yds. At this point, turn left by a telegraph pole and proceed by a short piece of stone wall on the left and over a badly overgrown stile to ascend the hillside with the hedge on the left. Beyond the brow of the hill at the corner of the field pass through the hedge and continue ahead for 200yds, passing a cricket ground on the left, to emerge on a minor road.

1.3 Abbey Lakes To Parbold Hill.
6 Miles. Route —·—·—·

Not to Scale

Wiggin Tree Restaurant

B.5239 STANDISH

PARBOLD

WALL ← Parbold Hill

stiles

Quarry

Cottage

┼┼┼┼┼┼ Railway

Leeds ╳ Liverpool canal.

River Douglas.

Farm →

Stile cottage

stiles

OLD Mine

Farm

stiles steps

Ashurst Beacon

Wire fence

stiles

hedge

stile

School Lane

WALTHEW GREEN

stile

Cottages

GOLF COURSE

Roby Mill

N

Deans Wood

M 6

Slab Bridge

Stream

Hedgerow.

Stream

Farm

Spencers Lane.

UPHOLLAND

A 577

Abbey Lakes Hotel

ORREL

10

Follow this road to the right and round a left hand bend for 200yds, and turn left where indicated by a P.F. sign opposite to a high stone wall around a house on the right. Proceed along this path between a wire fence on the right and trees on the left. Cross several stiles and a drive to a residence to skirt round a pond on the left to arrive at open land and a broad track leading to the right onto Ashurst Beacon *(Plate3)*.

As you leave the tower, bear right to the viewpoint (large inscribed stone) and continue down through woods by the eastern slope to a stile. Proceeding into the field follow the path to the right round the side of the field to cross another stile, and a small footbridge into another field.

With the hedge/fence on the left, walk round the edge of this field and down steps into a lane. Turn left on the lane and descending steeply on the metalled surface towards Banghams Farm. At the gateway to the farm at G.R.508083, turn left beside a P.F. sign near a white painted house opposite Banghams Farm entrance. You are now on a farm track as you cross a stile towards a wooded ravine. Do not enter this ravine but turn to the right and follow the track that descends into the valley. You arrive at a main road beside Lower House Farm. Outside the farm turn left for 100yds then right again at a P.F. sign opposite a large house.

Take the wide path that bears to the right, but where it turns sharply left, follow the track between hedgerows/fences to the right. Cross a stile then metal bridge over the River Douglas then cross the stone bridge over the Leeds & Liverpool Canal. Follow the winding track, cross a railway bridge then cross a lane by a stile followed by a kissing gate near a house. Ascend a steep path for approx. 400yds through a small wood to the B5239 road and viewpoint of Parbold Hill with The Wiggin Tree pub opposite.

Viewpoints: -

The view from Ashurst Beacon is limited by the close proximity of Harrock Hill to the north and Billinge Beacon to the south, nevertheless, on a clear day, the coastline from the Fylde to the Mersey and North Wales is clearly visible, as are the distant hills of Wales and the Central Pennines.

1.4 – Parbold Hill to Coppull Moor (5½miles)

Access: -

  The starting point for this section is the Wiggin Tree pub at the top of Parbold Hill. This lies within 1mile of the Wigan – Wrightington bus route at the Dicconson Arms near Dangerous Corner, and is approximately 1mile from the village and station of Parbold on the Wigan to Southport railway.

Route: -

  In front of the Wiggin Tree pub turn right for 100yds to a P.F. sign just past the far end of the pub car park and turn left. Walk on this track keeping a hedge to your left for 130yds then go through an opening on your left into a field. Walk now in the same direction keeping the hedge to your right then skirt clockwise round a pond, crossing a stile near the next large pond. Continue on a path towards a white painted house and a narrow metalled road that leads to the main road at Highmoor. Turn right for 180yds to The High Moor Restaurant. Just beyond this, turn left up the drive by the large tree towards Harrock Hall. Continue to a point where the concrete drive bends left down to Harrock Hall and take the P.F. off to the right, crossing a stile.

  You see a mast at the brow of the hill as you walk on a narrow path to the top. At the top, turn left by the side of the wood on a narrow path, crossing several stiles towards a small wood at G.R.513130. Walk around the left side of the wood crossing a stile then skirting the wood again, follow round the side of the field with the hedgerow on the right. You are now on Harrock Hill as you cross a stile into the main wood ahead onto a clockwise path through the wood to pass the site of the old windmill on your left.

  Continuing in an easterly direction, a grass track descends by the side of the wood to pass a farm on the left to join a lane which continues to descend, passing a house on the right to a T-junction further down. Turn right here for 50yds to a 5-bar gate on your left at G.R.517133, with a stile beside it. Walk now for 100yds to cross the field keeping a coppice and the hedgerow to your right and a small pond to your left. Take extra care with navigation here.

  Continue over a stile into the field on the right and down the field to the left with the hedgerow on the left. Where this hedgerow goes sharp left, the path continues straight ahead to the lowest part of the field, but due to ploughing it may be advisable to follow round the left hand edge of the field to the lowest point. Crossing a stile and a plank bridge at the lowest point of this field, continue ahead over a

1·4 PARBOLD HILL TO COPPULL MOOR.
5½ MILES.   ROUTE —·—·—

Not to Scale

COPPULL MOOR

NEW - SEVEN STARS INN

A49(T)

LANGTREE HALL
WEST - FARM

gate

STREAM

Stile & steps.
M6

Stile & Bridge.

MOTORWAY

SCARR BROOK

gate & stiles

Stile

Track.

BROADHURST LANE

B 52 50

Farm
Stile

ELEC - SUB - STN

BROADHURST

HEDGE

Path

Toogood farm

Cottages

FENCE

HEDGE.

Stiles

Stream

Footbridge

Field hedges

Stiles

LANE

EMBANKMENT & Stile

Gate

LANE

BOX

Path

Farms

stile 3

Stiles

gate

Poles, Stiles

B5239

PARBOLD HILL

Ruin of Windmill

High moor Restaurant.

hedge
Pond.

Wiggan Tree Restaurant.

HARROCK HILL

HARROCK HALL

farm.

HIGH MOOR

N

stile at the corner of the wood on the right, and a second stile onto a wide track by the side of the wood. You emerge on a road opposite Toogood Farm on Toogood Lane at G.R.525131. Turn right on the lane for 600yds to a P.F. sign just past the houses on higher ground ahead.

Turn left on the P.F. by the far side of a new home, walking generally in a northeasterly direction for 975yds. Walk now on a grass track in a straight line, passing a fishing lake to the road beyond (B5250) at Broadhurst. Turn right at the road, pass a playing field, you come into Mossy Lea. Continue to a metalled road on the left, which is Broadhurst Lane and walk along it.

After 300yds turn right on a narrow lane looking for P.F. sign on the corner. Ascend the lane, which turns into a track, following it along then over a stile into a large field at G.R.540130. Cross the field diagonally to a stile near a 5-bar gate, heading towards some trees. A gate is in front with the trees to your left. Go through the gate, turning right by the fence to the west side of Chisnall Wood. With the wood on the left, continue to a stile into the next field and along to a stile near the far end leading into the wood. Enter the wood, cross a brook then exit the wood over a stile to the bridge over the M6 motorway.

Cross the bridge then turn right over a stile beside a 5-bar gate. Follow track then just before you come to another stile beside a 5-bar gate ahead, look for another gate to the right of it. Cross there onto a worn grass track descending to Stars Brook. As you cross a stile the M6 is on your right. Cross the footbridge at the bottom and ascend the narrow path in the same direction on the other side. Take a sharp left turn 120yds up the field towards Langtree Old Hall Farm. Continue along the service road to the A49 at The New Seven Stars Inn.

Viewpoint: -
From the top of Harrock Hill the whole of the Lancashire coastline and the Bowland Fells used to be visible on a good day also the Lake District and Yorkshire Fells, together with the coastline and hills of Wales and the Isle of Anglesey, but most of this wide vista is now obscured by trees.

1.5 – Coppull Moor to Blackrod (5¼miles)

Access: -

Commencing at The New Seven Stars Inn 1¼miles north of Standish on the A49 trunk road, this section of the route lies on the Wigan-Preston bus route.

Route: -

Taking the broad track alongside the inn through a sand winning area and through an opening at the side of some metal gates, proceed for ¼mile to Hic-Bibi Brook *(Plate 4)*. You may see the spire of Standish church off to your right. Continue with the brook on the left for over ½mile, almost to the third wooden bridge over the brook, 350yds from the railway ahead. At this point, turn right and proceed on a field track, parallel with the railway, following a line of power cable poles up to some trees at G.R.567121. Walk to the left in front of the trees, crossing to a farm track at the far side of a clearing.

Continue ahead crossing a railway bridge before descending towards a row of houses on Platt Lane and passing The Crown Inn. Follow the road round up to the main A5106 road. Cross the main road and go through an opening beside a 5-bar gate onto a farm track. The path leads down to Worthington Lakes. Cross an iron stile and a footbridge, stay on the path then take a right fork, ascending by iron railings onto a path leading to a reservoir. Cross a stile in the corner leading down through Arley Wood.

Follow a path crossing a footbridge over the River Douglas and ascend a path ahead through trees *(Plate 5)* to the edge of Arley Golf Course. Follow the track round to the entrance beside Arley Hall at G.R.589107. Pass to the right of the hall now on a road, which soon bends left then right to cross a stone bridge over the Leeds-Liverpool Canal. Continue for ½mile along the lane crossing a disused railway and passing some houses and a farm until you reach a house called Hollinshead.

Turn left along Blundell Lane to ascend slightly then right on reaching the road by Gallaghers pub at Little Scotland. Continue down the hill for 170yds, to turn left just before the first bungalow on the left where there is a P.F. sign. Ascend the field with the hedgerow on the right then bear right, through an opening in the hedge that is directly across the field from Gallaghers pub. Cross three stiles initially heading towards the white farm ahead, which is Sibberings Farm. Look ahead for a stile in the far left corner of the field as you leave the farm to your right. This brings you onto a lane, which you cross,

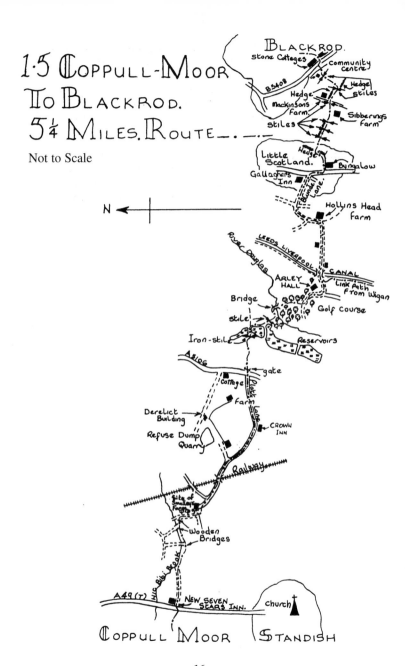

1·5 Coppull-Moor
To Blackrod.
5¼ Miles. Route _. _. _

Not to Scale

N ←

Blackrod.
Stone Cottages
Community Centre
B5408
Hedge Stiles
Hedge
Mackinsons Farm
Sibberings Farm
Stiles
Little Scotland.
Hedge
Bungalow
Gallaghers Inn
Bundel Lane.
Hollins Head Farm
Leeds Liverpool
River Douglas
Canal
Arley Hall
Link Path From Wigan
Bridge
Golf Course
Stile
Iron-stile
Reservoirs
A5106
gate
Cottage
Platt Lane
Farm
Derelict Building
Crown Inn
Refuse Dump
Quarry
Railway
Site of Smallware Factory
Wooden Bridges
River Bibi Brook
A49 (T)
New Seven Stars Inn.
Church
Coppull Moor
Standish

walking on another P.F. behind some buildings then bungalow's at G.R.615105, by the side of a field, to a stile on your left.

Cross the stile onto a tarmac path behind more bungalow's, taking you through a housing estate to a community centre in Blackrod. Continue a short distance to Vicarage Road at the main road junction. There are stone cottages at the far side.

Points of Interest: -

Arley Hall is of considerable historical interest since it is believed to be the oldest moated hall in the country. Although the date over the door is 1367, parts of the building reputedly date back to the twelfth century. Since the late 19th century, the hall has been in use as a clubhouse by the local golf club.

1.6 – Blackrod to Rivington (3miles)

Access: -

The final section of the route's first stage starts in the village of Blackrod, which is readily accessible by direct bus services from Chorley, Bolton and Wigan.

Route: -

Continuing from where the previous section finished on the B5408 in the centre of Blackrod Village, G.R.619106. Look for a P.F. sign at the side of the stone cottages opposite which leads to a stile. Crossing this stile, descend on a grass path *(Plate 6)* with panoramic views of Anderton services, Rivington Pike, the M61 and Winter Hill. Cross a further stile into a small piece of woodland, following the path round to Bank Houses and as you pass them, turn beside a sign for White Hall Lane. Descend a short, narrow path of cobbled stones to cross the A6 trunk road with care.

On the far side of the A6, continue through a kissing gate to cross a railway line then up to a bridge over the M61 motorway. When crossing the bridge there are services on your left should you need any supplies. Walk to the cattle grid over the bridge then turn right down a narrow tarmac farm lane to Anderton Old Hall Farm. Go through a small kissing gate and continue on a track to bypass the farm, walking closely to the left of farm buildings and over a small stile at the side of a white gate.

You walk on a metalled lane for 200yds then as the road bends left you turn right on a narrow path which swings round in the same direction as the road. Cross a small bridge with a waterfall on your left at G.R.630117, then pick up a track a short distance further on your left to take you along by the stream. Pass through a metal gate leading to some new houses and walk between them into a courtyard, turning left to the road.

Turn right on the dual carriageway, a sign nearby states 'Welcome to Horwich'. Cross the road there and ascend Dryfield Lane walking round a bend further on to Rivington Lodge. From here there are several routes into Rivington Village.

Direct: -

A P.B. sign just past the lodge leads on an obvious path left between fields. On reaching the road, bear left on the footpath, soon to arrive at the Lower Barn from where a path, which starts alongside the road, continues to Rivington Village.

1·6 BLACKROD TO RIVINGTON.
3 MILES. ROUTE —·—·—·—

Not to Scale

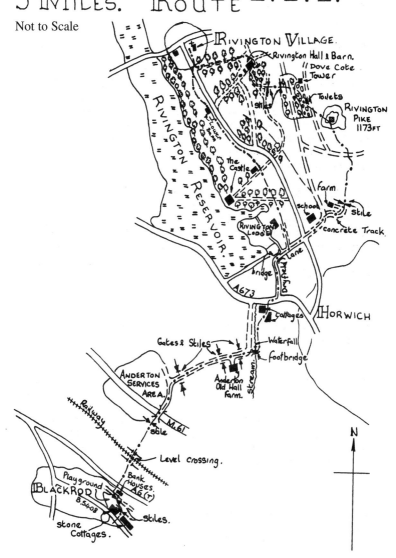

RIVINGTON VILLAGE.
Rivington Hall & Barn.
Dove Cote
Tower
Hall
Toilets
RIVINGTON PIKE 1173 FT
stiles
RIVINGTON RESERVOIR.
Lower Course
the Castle
farm
school
stile
RIVINGTON LODGE
concrete Track
Dryfield Lane
bridge
A 673
cottages
HORWICH
Gates & Stiles
Waterfall
footbridge
ANDERTON SERVICES AREA.
Anderton Old Hall Farm.
stream
Railway
M.61
stile
Level crossing.
N
Playground
Bank Houses A6 (T)
BLACKROD
B.5408
stiles.
stone Cottages.

19

Alternative: - (Taking in higher ground)

Continue to the end of Dryfield Lane and bearing right along the main park road for 50yds, take the track on the left outside the boundary fence of the school on the left. Beyond the school a concrete track bears right through an iron gate then back to ascend the hill. Where this track turns left into a farm, continue straight ahead along by the fence on the right, over a stile and across a field towards the stone tower on the top of Rivington Pike. Descending from the tower in a N.W. direction towards a stone building (toilets) follow the track to the left of these toilets through rhododendron gardens to the main staircase down from the Dove Cote Tower. Continue down this staircase through the gardens for 300yds in a W.N.W. direction, crossing a bridge over another broad track and, on reaching the bottom, bear right to a stile into a field. Climb this stile, cross the field and after climbing the stile on the other side, continue ahead on a track which bears slightly right to reach Rivington Hall and Barn within 250yds. From here, Rivington Village is reached by taking the track to the west from the back of the old Tithe Barn.

Viewpoints and Points of Interest: -

The view from Rivington Pike is somewhat restricted by the close proximity of the Billinge and Parbold Hills to the west and Winter Hill to the east. On a clear day, however, it is possible to see the southern fells of the Lake District to the north and across the vast expanse of the Cheshire Plain to the south.

At Rivington Lower Barn there is a Park's Centre together with toilets and a café that is normally open for refreshments between 10-00am and 5-00pm.

STAGE 2 – RIVINGTON TO WHALLEY (24½miles)

2.1 – Rivington to Abbey Village (9miles)

Access: -

The first section of this stage of the route commences at Rivington Village, which is accessible by bus from Chorley and Horwich.

Route: -

Proceed across the village green passing the Post Office and church on the right and, descending steps, cross a road to pass through a kissing gate (next to a P.F. sign) in the wall opposite. Continue along a field path, descend stone steps and bearing slightly right, pass over a stile onto a narrow path alongside a stream on the left. Crossing the next stile, turn left along a narrow lane for 50yds, then right, through an opening next to a 5-bar gate to take you along a broad stony track, which rises to run along the left side of the Yarrow Reservoir. Halfway up the path forks, bear left descending the winding path to the main road and bridge beside Anglezarke Reservoir. Turn right, walk along the pavement for 280yds to the junction.

Turning left at the road junction, signposted 'Anglezarke and Heapey', leave the road after a short distance and continue ahead, with Anglezarke Reservoir on your left, through a gate onto a tarmac footpath. Keeping to this undulating path continue alongside the reservoir for ½mile, passing through an opening, then ascend an embankment passing High Bullough Reservoir on your right. At a 5-bar gate the path descends to a kissing gate, now on a stony track. At a stile, cross onto a narrow path across a field keeping the Anglezarke reservoir on your left. Cross another two stiles on the bracken lined path onto a road.

Proceeding diagonally left across the road through a kissing gate, continue along a track for ¾mile with the River Goit off to your left as you walk to the cricket field and pavilion at White Coppice, G.R.620190, *(Plate 7)*. With these on the left continue ahead on a distinct path, which veers right as it climbs steeply up the hillside from White Coppice *(Plate 8)*. At a fork in the path signposted 'Brinscall', turn right, still ascending a steep, rutted path towards Great Hill, which you should see ahead.

Continue on the narrow path passing several ruined farm-steads and a coppice. Arriving on Great Hill (1200ft), there is a 4-way wind shelter on the summit. On leaving the summit, bear 67°M

2·1 Rivington To Abbey Village.
9 Miles.   Route —·—·—.
Not to Scale

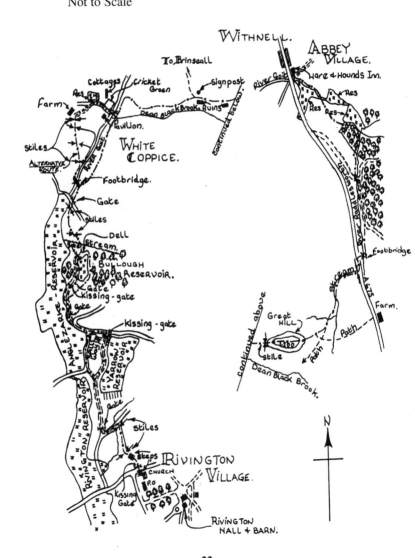

Withnell.

Abbey Village.

To Brinscall

Signpost

Hare & Hounds Inn.

Res

Res Res

River Goit

Dean Black Brook. Ruins

Cottages   Cricket Green

Farm

Res

Pavilion.

Continued below

White Coppice.

Stiles

Alternative Route.

River Goit

Footbridge.

Gate

Stiles

Dell

Stream.

Bullough Reservoir.

Gate

Kissing - gate

Gate

Kissing - gate

Anglezarke Reservoir.

Footbridge

Stream

A675

Farm.

Continued above

Great Hill

1249

stile

Path

Path

Dean Black Brook.

Yarrow Reservoir.

Gate

Rivington Reservoir.

Stiles

Steps

Church

P.O.

Kissing Gate

Rivington Village.

Rivington Hall & Barn.

N

22

following the sign towards Darwin Tower, which you may see in the direction you are heading. Descend the hillside for 460yds, looking for a feint path on left, which swings north then east until it reaches a stream. Follow downhill, first on left then right to turn into a stony track that continues to follow the stream to a small bridge, emerging on the A675 at a point ¼mile below a farm.

Crossing the road, turn left, and in 100yds take the P.F. into the wood on the right. After 30yds this crosses a small stream and turns sharp left to follow the lower of two tracks alongside the stream, which cascades over a narrow rocky bed. In 300yds the path climbs sharply to the right to merge into a stony track that continues to follow the stream to a small bridge.

Cross this bridge, turn right through a kissing gate and proceed with stream on right. After steps, take track to left away from the stream, passing through a wood to a road from the dam of the reservoir on the right.

Continue along this road and 150yds from a gate ahead take the path on the right. This continues with another reservoir on the right to a footbridge, which you cross onto a road. Proceed left to cross another footbridge over the spillway, and ahead with a house on the left to the service road which, to the right *(Plate 9)* leads to the Hare & Hounds at Abbey Village.

Viewpoint: -
The only vantage points of any significance on this section of the route is on the hillside at White Coppice *(Plate 8)* and Great Hill, from where the view encompasses the Fylde, including Blackpool Tower, and the fells of North and Central Lancashire.

2.2 – Abbey Village – Mellor (8miles)

Access: -

      Abbey Village lies on the A675 and is accessible by public transport from Blackburn, Chorley and Wigan. At the time of writing this guide, the section to the motorway bridge is being re-signposted in parts and may for a time be difficult to follow.

Route: -

      Starting from the Hare & Hounds Inn, leave the A675 to the south of the car park by a track leading to Red Lea Farm. After 350yds, take the path diagonally off to the right descending steps to regain the farm track in a narrow valley. Passing over a stile alongside the stream, turn left and proceed with the stream on the right to cross a stile into a wooded area. Follow the path ahead with the stream and lake on the right to a lane above the dam.

      Turn up this lane to a house and proceed through a gap in the fence on the right of the house, along a field below the old railway embankment. At the end of the field, a stile and footbridge lead into a wood. Proceed ahead on the ill defined footpath for 250yds and cross the railway onto a rising track which, if followed by the right-hand fence line, leads to a marked path with a pond on the left. From here continue straight ahead and on reaching a wood cross a stile into the field and continue alongside the wood to pass over another stile and under the M65 motorway. Continue ahead, turning left at the far side under power lines at G.R.644245 and ascend the field to an opening at the top left corner. Turn right at the top to descend the field to the Leeds-Liverpool Canal in the valley.

      On reaching the canal, cross the bridge, turn left on the towpath for 1200yds, passing under two bridges to arrive at Riley Green opposite The Boatyard Inn. Approximately 120yds before the bridge, turn right on an overgrown path, passing masts to emerge on the A6061 beside cottages.

      Turn left for 100yds on a footpath, cross the road to go down a lane. After ¼mile, where lane veers sharp left to cottages, go through kissing gate on right. Descend to River Darwen, through gate, before turning acutely left. Cross a ladder stile following path with river on right at G.R.630258. Pass beneath a railway viaduct, emerging on a minor road near an old mill.

      Continue past several houses and a row of cottages to a 3-storey house beside a right hand bend. Turn right there down a lane to regain the river at a humpback bridge. Turn left at the side of the bridge, walking along the riverbank at Hoghton Bottoms to emerge at

2·2 Abbey-Village-Mellor 8 Miles. — Route —·——

Not to Scale

Skiles.

Hacking House Farm

stile

PRESTON

A677(?)

BLACKBURN

ARLEY BROOK

ARLEY FARM

Stiles.

MIDDLE SHORROCK HEY FARM

Cottages

WILMAR LODGE

Tree & Telegraph Pole

CLOG & BILLYCOCK INN

Stiles.

CLOSE FARM

Wall

Wall

Stile

Houses

Stile

Scout Huts

QUARRIES

Footbridge

HOGHTON BOTTOMS

Stile.

MAIDEN Ho.

Cottage (Teas)

BILLINGE HILL.

PRESTON

RAILWAY

Cottage

OLD MILL.

HOGHTON TOWER

VIADUCT

N

Cottages(?)

RIVER DARWEN

Cottages(?)

Stiles.

RILEY GREEN Cottages

A6061

BLACKBURN

LEEDS-LIVERPOOL CANAL

Boat Yard

STANWORTH FARM

Pond

BRICK WORKS

A675

PAPER MILLS

SHAW LEDGE(?)

M65

RESERVOIR

Stiles.

Cottage

RED LEA FARM

HARE & HOUNDS INN

ABBEY VILLAGE

RODDLESWORTH RESERVOIR

WITHNELL.

RAKE BROOK RESERVOIR

BOLTON

Plate 1
St Helens Canal - The path ahead

Plate 2
Billinge Hill in the distance

Plate 3
The path to Ashurst Beacon

Plate 4
A winters day along Hic Bibi Brook

a girder footbridge. Turning right away from the river towards Lower Park Farm, pass in front of the farm building, turning left at the far side to regain the river again, passing a scout hut on your right. The path soon ascends steeply through a wooded area with a ravine on the left. After 300yds, bear right for 100yds along a short wooded ravine, which you cross. From here the path climbs out of the ravine towards a stile at the right hand side of a stone wall at G.R.633277.

Cross the stile, and an open field to pass in front of Close Farm (house). Passing it, cross a stile on right to take you by the side of the house and a hedge line. Bear right, round a spring into the next field then left to a minor road ahead. Cross the road towards Maiden House Farm where the track bends right to farm buildings, take the track bearing left towards a 5-bar gate. Cross the field to an opening at far left corner then cross the next field to a stile at the right of a white painted house, leading into a wooded area.

Entering the wood, turn left for 160yds to ascend to houses with garages on the right. Look for a small P.F. post on your right, just before the garages and turn right to ascend the hillside over two stiles. Continue towards Billinge Hill *(Plate 2),* (a wooded hill) and before it a smaller hill with good views all round. A small pond in a former quarry is there. Walk to a fence and stile past the smaller hill G.R.649279, then turn left to another stile 100yds further. Cross the stile, descending to the Clog and Billycock Inn.

Cross the road diagonally right, from the inn and climb the stile at the left side of the garages behind the houses, following the path down the field, bearing slightly right at the telegraph pole to descend the hill to a road junction. Proceed down the lane opposite heading due north, to the last house where a stile on the left by the fence gives access to a field. Descend to Arley Brook at the bottom, crossing it to Arley Farm.

Cross the farmyard to a gate in the diagonal corner and walk along the lane the busy A677 road. Turn right for 150yds then left along the service road to Hacking House Farm. Keep to the right of the farm, passing through two gates before ascending at the far side by a line of trees to the left. Cross a small footbridge then bear 348°M to ascend an old lane which emerges at the lower end of Mellor near a gate on the left where the P. F. runs through the rear of a house garden, to emerge on the road.

Viewpoint: -
Distant views are generally precluded on this section, but there are several points where there are extensive views of the local countryside, the most noteworthy being the ridge leading towards Billinge Hill.

2.3 – Mellor – Whalley (7½miles)

Access: -

    The village of Mellor lies 3miles N.W. of Blackburn and less than a mile north of the A677 trunk road, along which there are regular bus services connecting Preston, Blackburn, Bolton, Burnley, Clitheroe and Skipton.

Route: -

    Starting on the south side of Mellor at G.R. 654305 follow the road round the east side of the village to Hob Green Road. Walk up to the Methodist Church at the top. Turn right; along the lane, passing The Traders Arms on your right, to the crossroads. Turn left along a lane and where the road bears left in front of a cottage, go over the stile on the right beyond the cottage. Climb the hill behind, keeping a wall on the left, pass over another stile, to the 'trig' point on the top of Mellor Moor 725ft.

    Leave the summit of the moor by a stile at the corner of a wire fence; proceed over several stiles diagonally down fields and 150yds from cottages look for a small stile to the right of a field entrance. Cross into a field, to emerge on a minor road to the right of a row of cottages. Turn left in front of the cottages for 15yds then cross a footbridge into a garden on the right. Turn left at far side of garden following arrow on tree. Nearing the house, turn right between trees and pass over a stile to the left of an old iron gate. Turn left to follow the tree line and stream off to your left.

    Cross a stile and walk diagonally down next field. Gradually leave the stream on left and cut across three field boundaries to pass over two stiles between holly bushes. Cross next field diagonally right then over another stile between another two holly bushes. Continue diagonally downhill, past two large oak trees on the right, towards Midge Hall Farm, but 60yds before the farm turn right to ascend to far left corner of the wooded area. Here there is a well-hidden stile between holly trees. Proceed over this onto a lane.

    Turn left then immediately right on a grassy track through trees to a gate and stile into a field. Cut straight across this field to a stile and footbridge keeping to a thin line of bushes on the right in the next field. Turn right for 110yds and left at far side of Hagg's Hall Farm, emerging on the road to the right of the farm buildings. Continue along the farm road to Ramsgreave Hall, following the access road to pass several conversions and new houses. Past last house on left in lane, turn left to pass white painted house with a stile ahead. Cross to follow a field path with a fence on the right and a capped reservoir beyond. Near the end of the reservoir, bear left down a field towards a pylon and Jersey farm. Pass over stile by farm at lower corner of field and continue along farm track. On reaching the road turn left.

Plate 5
The path to Arley Hall between the Golf Course

Plate 6
The panoramic view across to Rivington

Plate 7
Stopping to check the map at White Coppice

Plate 8
Looking back on the ascent at White Coppice

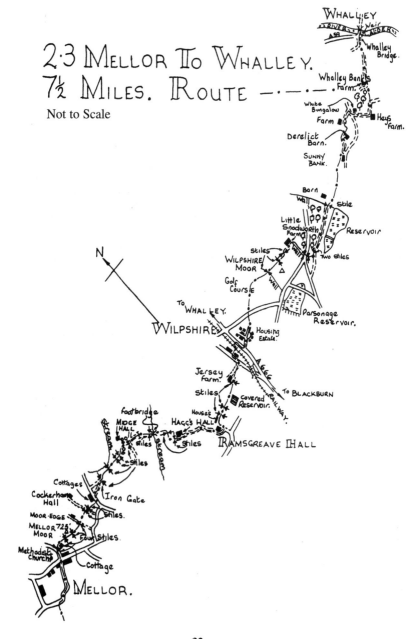

2·3 MELLOR TO WHALLEY.
7½ MILES. ROUTE —·—·—

Not to Scale

WHALLEY

RIVER CALDER

Weir

A59

Whalley Bridge.

Whalley Banks Farm.

White Bungalow Farm

Hays Farm.

Derelict Barn.

SUNNY BANK.

Barn

Wall

Stile

Little Snodworth Farm

Reservoir

Stiles

WILPSHIRE MOOR

Two Stiles

N

Golf Course

Wall

Parsonage Reservoir.

TO WHALLEY.

WILPSHIRE

Housing Estate.

A666

Jersey Farm.

TO BLACKBURN

Stiles

Covered Reservoir.

RAILWAY.

Footbridge

Stream

MIDGE HALL

Houses

HAGG'S HALL

Stiles

Stiles

Stream

RAMSGREAVE HALL

Stiles

Cottages

Cockerham Hall

Iron Gate

MOOR·EDGE

Stiles.

MELLOR 725' MOOR

Four Stiles.

Methodist Church

Cottage

MELLOR.

32

Walk 150yds along Primrose Terrace then right up a footpath by a white house, ascending behind houses then under a railway line. Walk up steps and on a track to the left then right onto the A666 road. Turn right along this road for 100yds; follow the dark, narrow rising path to left between the gardens of two mansions. Continue to right on path between gardens of two houses onto next estate road above then straight ahead on a path between houses 15 & 17 to the top. Cross a stile on left and follow path anti-clockwise round field, crossing to rear of end house at far side. Walk behind to emerge on Hollowhead Lane opposite Wilpshire Golf Course.

Cross the road and continue over the golf course; the footpath being marked by black and white posts; to a stile in a wall above the 8th tee. Follow straight across next field, keeping 'trig' point on top of a hill off to the right, walk to a stile in lower left side of the field. Pass over several stiles keeping a wall on the left, to Little Snodworth Farm. Proceed through the farmyard and turn right by the wall beyond, to emerge over another stile onto a minor road at a Y-junction. Cross road and a stile opposite, also a second stile across the field beyond, turn left and after 100yds, fork right to follow the track, with a wood to the left and Dean Clough Reservoir below to the right.

On nearing a point above the dam of the reservoir, proceed through a kissing gate, turn right for 100yds to a post with a yellow arrow then turn left, to the left of a water pipe at G.R.717335 at same contour level, to join a track below Sunny Bank with the fence line on the right. Continue ahead in the same direction keeping the fence/hedge line on the right to a stile onto a walled track rising from cottages below Sunny Bank on Shawcliffe Lane.

Continue up this track through a 5-bar gate to the ruins of farm buildings and pass through another 5-bar gate towards Lower White Carr ahead. Descend the field to the rear of a farm and cross the stile between the first farm buildings onto the service road, to emerge on a minor road. Turn right for 50yds, then left by a white bungalow down Berry's Lane to Heys Farm. Turn left before the farm, proceed for 350yds, and where the track bears sharp right, ascend the stony path to the left up to Whalley Banks Farm. Walk along Dean Lane into Whalley Banks, branching right further on, to descend to the River Calder by the bridge at Whalley *(Plate 10)*.

Viewpoint: -
This section provides extensive views to Pendle Hill and Longridge Fell with glimpses of the Bowland and Yorkshire Fells and the prominent landmarks of Winter Hill T.V. mast and Blackpool Tower.

Plate 9
Approaching the Hare and Hounds
by the reservoir track near Abbey Village

Plate 10
The path by the River Calder at Whalley

Plate 11
Pendle Hill Summit and the extensive view with
Barley Village just over the hill to the right

Plate 12
Thornton-in-Craven church and the last field!

STAGE 3 – WHALLEY TO THORNTON-IN-CRAVEN (17½miles)

3.1 – Whalley to Barley or Downham (7½/9miles)

Access: -
    The final stage of the route commences at Whalley, which lies on the Preston – Skipton and Bolton - Blackburn - Burnley – Clitheroe bus routes.

Route: -
    Commencing from the bridge over the River Calder and walking towards Whalley, turn right at the footpath sign opposite along Calder Vale, and follow the river path upstream *(Plate 10),* until it bears left over a stile. Continue with a hedge on the left and a farm on the right and cross another stile onto the A671. After crossing this road, turn right and then left over a stile into a field where a rising path, bearing right, leads to a further stile and onto the embankment of the Whalley by-pass link road from the A671 near traffic lights. Cross to the entrance of Springwood Picnic Area and in the corner near the lights is a stile to cross.

    Your path now ascends the left side of a golf course and a wood for 300yds to a footbridge and stile in the hedge on the left, which leads into a field at G.R.743361. Proceed diagonally up the field to the top left hand corner with a coppice surrounded by a wall on the right. From this point three stiles are crossed in quick succession to emerge into another field from where you continue ahead but slightly left onto a farm track. Follow this track keeping the coppice now to the right.

    Walk round to join a metalled lane, turning left for ¾mile, passing Wiswell Moor Farm on the right to Wiswell Moor Houses further ahead on the left. A mast is on the hillside to the left. From here keep ahead through a gate and along the track a further 1¼miles, emerging on the Nick 'o' Pendle Road just ½mile above Sabden Village in the valley on the right. Turning left, follow the road verge to the crown of the hill from where a broad track on the right leads to open moorland. Continue along this well defined path for a mile or so on a general bearing of 54°M, rising gradually all the way with good views over Clitheroe to the left. The worn path continues generally in a N.N.E. direction towards Ogden Clough where it joins a well-defined path on the left of the stream. After proceeding upstream for approximately ½mile, cross it and continue in an E.N.E. direction on a slabbed path to the cairn and 'trig' point at the top of Pendle Hill *(Plate 11).* On leaving the summit, proceed in a N. direction towards a gate in a wall.

3·1 Whalley To Barley
7½ - 9 Miles   (OR) Downham
Route —·—·—

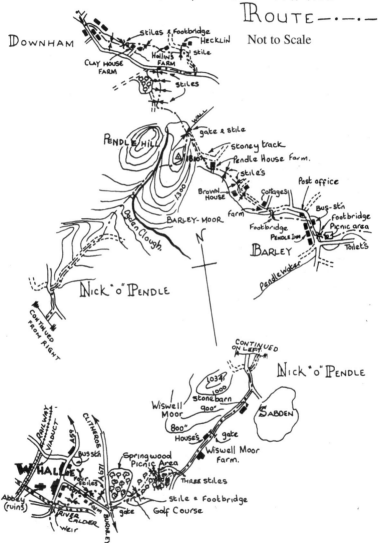

Downham

Stiles & Footbridge
Hecklin
Not to Scale

Hollins Farm
stile

Clay House Farm

stiles

Pendle Hill
gate & stile

WALL

stoney track
△1810'
Pendle House Farm.

stile's
Post office

Brown House
Cottages
Bus-st'n
△1320
farm
Footbridge
Picnic area

Barley-Moor
Footbridge
Pendle Inn
Barley
Toilet's

Ogden Clough
Pendle Water

N

Nick "o" Pendle

CONTINUED FROM RIGHT

CONTINUED ON LEFT
Nick "o" Pendle

1034'
1000'
stonebarn
Wiswell Moor
900'
Saboen
800'
Houses
gate
Wiswell Moor Farm.

Railway Viaduct
A671 Clitheroe
Bus st'n
Springwood Picnic Area
Three stiles
Whalley
Four stiles
A671 Burnley
stile & Footbridge
Golf Course
Abbey (ruins)
River Calder
gate
Weir

37

Descent to Barley: -

Approximately 100yds. from the gate in the wall, pick up and follow the wide stony track on the right, which doubles back and descends in steps to Pendle House Farm. Go through a kissing gate at the bottom then bear to the right behind Pendle House Farm to another kissing gate. After passing through this gate, descend by a stone wall on the left and pass into the next field to continue ahead to another gate. Veering diagonally right down the next field, pass behind Ings Head Farm with a cottage on the left to emerge onto a lane. Turn right to Brown House then left in front of it. Descend by the stream to Ing Ends to join a lane. After 50yds down the path to the left, cross a footbridge over the stream on the right then continue to the left, emerging in Barley by the stream near the Post Office. Turning right through the village, proceed past a restaurant and the Pendle Inn to the car park, toilets and picnic area.

Descent to Downham: -

Pass over the stile in the wall just below the gate and follow the path ahead. After ¾mile of gradual descent, the path turns at right angles and continues across open moorland and several stiles to emerge on a road to the right of a small wood. Turning right, walk up the road and take the first farm track on the left. After 300yds, pick up a footpath on the left, which continues, to Clay House Farm. Pass behind the farm and diagonally left across a field to a stile and wooden footbridge. Crossing the bridge, follow the field track with the stream on the right to the picturesque village of Downham.

Viewpoints: -

Following such a gradual climb, the view from the top of Pendle Hill 1831ft *(Plate 11)* comes as something of a surprise with a dramatic 1000ft drop to the village of Barley and its reservoirs below. In addition, on a clear day, the view takes in the fells of Longridge, Beacon and Bowland, and the distant Yorkshire Hills of Ingleborough and Pen-y-Ghent.

3.2 – Barley to Thornton-in-Craven (10miles)

Access: -

The isolated village of Barley, which lies in the shadow of Pendle, may be reached by an infrequent bus service from Burnley, or a more frequent service from Nelson.

Route: -

Continuing from the car park where there are public toilets and a water tap, leave from the far end and proceed along the track between cottages, keeping Pendle Water on your right. You come to some newly built cottages further along where you turn left following a signpost and passing Holly House on your left on the corner. Follow the lane round between houses then ascend the minor road to a small brick transformer or pump house on the right at G.R.832404.

Pass over a stile behind the pump house into a wood, following the path through the wood and passing a school off to the left. Cross a stream as you head to a field stile ahead and walk diagonally to a wall of a residence and a stile. Proceed onto the service road by a series of stiles to the rear of the residence and on reaching a minor road, turn left up the hill. Where the road bears left, take the track on the right walking to a stone barn cottage. Keep to the left of the cottage through a 5-bar gate then through small double metal gates to ascend a grass track. Reaching the far end of the fence line, turn right towards a distant tower keeping a wood to your right.

Gradually descend the hillside, crossing over two stiles by a stone barn. Continue following the path in line with the tower to a gate into a forestry plantation. Keep descending the hillside bearing slightly left through pine trees to a stone stile into another pine wood plantation. Cross another stile still descending on a feint path at G.R.848416, to the stream at the bottom. Cross and walk to a gate at the far right corner of the field, crossing another stream there onto a path over a field and through a wood to steps up to a bridge.

Descending steps on the opposite side of the road, continue over a stile and across fields, with the stream on the right to just before a large house at Lower Admergill. Cross a footbridge on your right then turn left to emerge to the right of the house on a service road. Turn left along the service road passing a farm and keeping Admergill Water on your right. Where the road bends left, go over a stile by a 5-bar gate keeping the stream still on right and cross several stiles towards a white public house on the hillside ahead. When you come to two stiles beside each other, take the right one to ascend the hillside diagonally towards a stone stile by a gate onto the A682 road above.

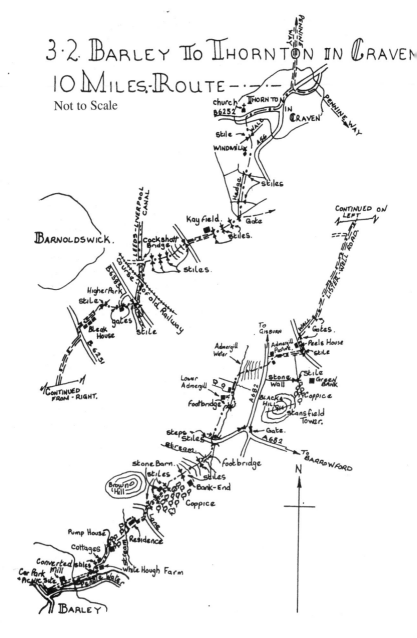

3.2. Barley To Thornton In Craven

10 Miles. Route —·—·—

Not to Scale

PENNINE WAY

church
B6252
THORNTON IN CRAVEN
PENNINE WAY

stile
WALL
Age

WINDMILL

Hedge
stiles

LEEDS LIVERPOOL CANAL

Kay field.
Gate
stiles.

CONTINUED ON LEFT

BARNOLDSWICK.

Cockshott Bridge

stiles.

LISTER WELL ROAD

Course of old Railway

Higher Park
stile
gates
Bleak House
stile
B 6251
CONTINUED FROM · RIGHT.

To GISBURN

WALL
Gates.
Admergill Pasture.
Peels House
stile

Admergill Water

stone wall
Stile
Green Bank
Coppice

Lower Admergill
A 682
BLACK HILL
Footbridge
Stansfield Tower.

steps
stiles
stream
Gate.
A 682
To BARROWFORD

footbridge

Stone Barn.
stiles
stiles
Bank-End
Browns Hill
Coppice

Pump House
Lane
Residence

Cottages
stream
Converted Mill
stiles
White Hough Farm
Car Park
·Picnic Site
Pendle Water
BARLEY

N

40

Turn left along the road for 10yds then right over another stone stile to ascend a field diagonally left to a house and farm at Admergill Pasture. Continue in an easterly direction with the properties, followed by a depression, on the left for 300yds to arrive at two stiles near each other in a stone wall. Cross right hand stile to walk 150yds between stone walls with Peel's House (white house) off to your left. On reaching a minor road, turn left for 200yds and pass the house on the left at G.R.864432. Follow the path through gate on right. After crossing a field and passing through a gate you are on Lister Well Road (track), which continues ahead for 1½miles before descending by a concrete section to the main B6251 road near Barnoldswick.

Cross the busy road with care, turning left then second right onto a bridleway. Continue for 280yds, passing houses on the right, to a P.F. and stile on the right to descend diagonally over several fields and stiles to a bridge over the Leeds-Liverpool Canal which you should see below. Cross a stile onto the B6383 road 100yds from the bridge over the canal. Walk across the bridge; turn right to descend the embankment to proceed along the canal towpath underneath the road. On reaching an arched bridge over the canal, leave the canal by the footpath on the right, crossing two or three stiles until the ground begins to rise sharply. At this point, bear slightly left to ascend the hill to the left of the ravine to a stile onto a minor road.

Cross the road, and proceed along the farm access road opposite to the farm ahead. Pass in front of the farm, continuing ahead over several stiles until you come to two stiles beside each other. Take the left stile to cross diagonally over more fields towards a bend in the A56 main road. Pass a disused metal windmill on your left then veer north, ascending to a stile near a farm. Cross the service road into an open field. The path continues across this field *(Plate 12)* to the final stile of the route, which is directly opposite the church on the B6252 on the outskirts of the village of Thornton-in-Craven. Turning right for 500yds to the 'T' junction and left for 300yds into the village of Thornton itself marks the end of the Lancashire Trail.

The Way Ahead: -
From here there are bus services for return to Skipton, Blackburn, Preston, Southport, Liverpool, Burnley, Bolton and Manchester. For those wishing to continue, the Pennine Way to the north connects with the Dales Way, Coast to Coast and The Pennine Link Footpath Routes, giving access to Kirk Yetholm in Scotland, St. Bees on the Cumbrian coast, Ravenscar on the Yorkshire coast, Keswick in Cumbria, and Ilkley in West Yorkshire.

4.0 – LINK PATHS

4.1 – Wigan to Arley Hall (4miles)

Access: -

The start of this link path is close to the centre of Wigan and within ½mile of railway and bus stations.

Route: -

Commencing near to the entrance of the Tesco supermarket, follow the path between the supermarket on the left and the River Douglas on the right to cross the river just beyond. Turning left, continue up the valley for ½mile with the river on the left. Descending steps on entering a wooded area, cross a small stream from the right and turn right to join a broad track, which in 600yds crosses the cutting of a disused railway line. After a further ½mile through the wood, the track reaches a bridge over the Leeds-Liverpool Canal. At this point the route leaves the track, which continues towards Haigh Hall, and follows the towpath of the canal in a northerly direction for 2miles, via Red Rock, to Arley Hall where the main trail is joined, (section 1.5 Coppull Moor to Blackrod).

Points of Interest: -

Haigh Hall - The history of this hall and the surrounding area is both long and varied. The name 'Haigh' comes from an Anglo-Saxon word meaning 'enclosure' and in early days it would have been a clearing in the forest where people lived, grazed their cattle and grew crops for their own use. The hall in those days would have been a simple structure with rudimentary furnishings.

During the following centuries the hall has been rebuilt to match the current styles and has seen many events of historical importance and masters from many different families. The present hall was built between the years 1830 and 1849 under the direction of its owner the 24th Earl of Crawford, who drew up his own plans and supervised much of the building. The sand stone for the hall was quarried at nearby Parbold and brought to the hall by canal.

In its varied history, the hall has been used for many purposes. During the War of 1914-1918 it was used as a military hospital. In 1947 the hall and grounds were purchased by Wigan Corporation and made available to the public. Since then additional leisure facilities have been added.

4.1 - Wigan to Arley Hall (4 miles)

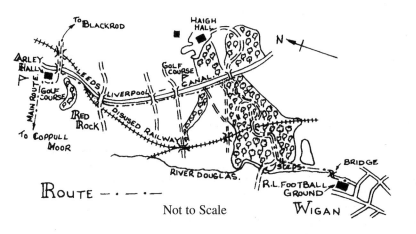

Route — . — . —

Not to Scale

4.2 - Bolton to Rivington (5 miles)

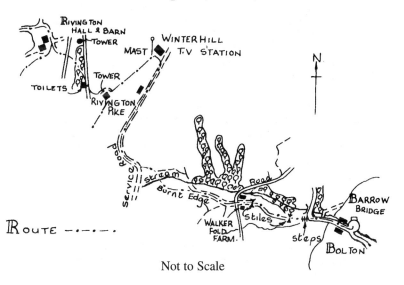

Route — . — . —

Not to Scale

43

4.2 – Bolton to Rivington (5miles)

Access: -

     The starting point is Barrow Bridge on the northwest side of Bolton, which is the terminus of a bus route.

Route: -

     Starting from the bus terminus, proceed up the road between cottages with the stream on the right. At the point where the road bears right over a bridge continue with the stream on the right, and climb the steps ahead to emerge into a field. Keeping straight on, pass over the stile leading into the next field with a low wall on the left. Proceed to Walkers Fold where a step stile leads onto a short lane, which emerges between the old farm and a number of cottages onto a moorland road.

     After crossing the road, proceed up the lane opposite onto the hillside where the track levels out and continues forward with a wood stretching down into the valley on the right. On a clear day the television mast on Winter Hill may be seen ahead to the right. Beyond the wood the path rises for ½mile as it proceeds along Burnt Edge. Subsequently, the track bears right then left to follow a defile, which rises onto the road leading to the television station on Winter Hill.

     On reaching the television tower itself, turn left on bearing 245°M to Rivington Pike. From this point continue down through the terraced gardens in Leverhulme Park to Rivington Hall and Barn, which is the start of stage 2 of the main route.

Viewpoint: -

     The top of Winter Hill provides an extensive view of the Lancashire coastline to the northwest with Morecambe Bay and the southern Lake District fells beyond. To the north and northeast can be seen the Lancashire and Yorkshire fells whilst immediately below lies the village of Belmont. The view to the south is across the Cheshire Plain and extends between the sprawling conurbations of Greater Manchester and Merseyside.

4.3 - Burnley to Barley (6miles)

Access: -

  The starting point is the Central Railway Station, which is within ½mile of Burnley town centre.

Route: -

  Leaving the station car park, follow the tarmac path between Sainsburys and the station across an open, grassed area towards houses. After 200yds, fork right along the cutting of an old railway track, passing under two bridges and through trees with a stream on the right and playing fields beyond. On approaching the aqueduct of the Leeds-Liverpool Canal, ascend the steps on the left to gain the towpath, which is followed to the left. After passing under five bridges, the canal sweeps first to the right away from the railway then back to the left under the railway and a pipe bridge.

  Continue along the towpath for just over ½mile, leaving the last housing estate behind on your left, turn left over a stile by a canal bridge, and follow down the field towards Pendle Water. Turning right continue along the path upstream to a stile giving access to a foot-bridge across to a house. Turning right in front of the house proceed over a stile then along a cinder track with Pendle Water on the right.

  After passing underneath motorway bridges, the track emerges onto the old Montford Road by a farm and cottages. Continuing to the left for a short distance, follow a footpath sign right, in front of the cottages and a bungalow. The track ascends through woods and away from the river, over two cattle grids and straight on (not on tarmac track to left) towards Old Laund Hall Farm. Proceed with farm to right and woods on left along the track, which rises to an iron gate and a kissing gate. Just before this iron gate there is a stile in the fence on the left, go over this stile and with the hedgerow on the right continue across fields and stiles until the B6247 road is reached.

  Crossing this road, climb the steps and stile on the opposite side and continue to the rear gardens of houses. At this point turn left and proceed with the houses on the right and after a short distance emerge by the White Swan Inn in the village of Wheatley Lane.

  Turning right and then left by the side of the White Swan, ascend a narrow road past a large new house and go straight ahead through a wooden gate into a field behind two semi-detached houses. Proceed up the field, over a stone stile and along a path between hedges onto Noggarth Road by a residence on the right.

4.3 Burnley To Barley
6 Miles
Route ·—·—·—
Not to Scale

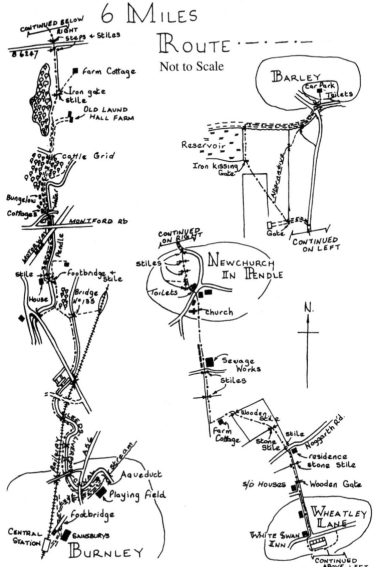

CONTINUED BELOW RIGHT
Steps + Stiles
B 6247
Farm Cottage
Iron gate stile
OLD LAUND HALL FARM
Cattle Grid
Bungalow Cottages
MONTFORD RD
Pendle Water
Stile
Footbridge + Stile
House
Bridge No 135
A 56
Leeds + Liverpool
Stream
Aqueduct
Playing Field
Footbridge
CENTRAL STATION
SAINSBURYS
BURNLEY

BARLEY
Car Park
Toilets
Reservoir
Iron kissing Gate
Newchurch
Gate
CONTINUED ON LEFT

CONTINUED ON RIGHT
Stiles
NEWCHURCH IN PENDLE
Toilets
church
Sewage Works
Stiles
N.
Wooden Stile
Farm Cottage
stile
Stone Stile
Noggarth Rd.
residence
stone stile
s/o Houses
Wooden Gate
WHEATLEY LANE
WHITE SWAN INN
CONTINUED ABOVE LEFT

Cross the road, and over a stile on the left hand side of a gate and continue up the field with the hedgerow on the right, to a stone stile. From this stile the path goes behind the farm cottage then across the field to a wooden stile opposite, before descending to a further stile giving access to a lane. Proceed across the lane between a sewage works on the right and a bungalow on the left and ascend the field path to the right of the churchyard to emerge in the village of Newchurch-in-Pendle.

Taking the ascending footpath to the left of the public toilets, continue over a stile and straight ahead, ignoring a stile on the left, to pass over two more stiles with hawthorn bushes on the left and a third stile onto the road. Bearing left along the road for 40yds, fork left along a cinder track, pass through a gate and fork immediately right in a north-westerly direction, leaving the cinder track and crossing fields towards the barrage of a reservoir below. Passing through gaps in two walls, descend to an iron kissing gate, cross the barrier of the reservoir and after climbing a stile by a gate, turn right along the track which joins with the main route in the village of Barley.

Points of Interest: -

The village of Newchurch–in–Pendle figures prominently in the history of witchcraft, which was practiced extensively during the seventeenth century in this area. Numerous members of the Nuttall family lie in the churchyard, probably relatives of the infamous Mistress Alice Nuttall who, along with eight other witches, was sentenced to death at the Lancaster Assize on Wednesday 19th August 1612, and subsequently hanged. Note the 'Eye of God' on the wall of the church tower, set there to ward off evil spirits.

4.4 – Downham to Sawley (2miles)

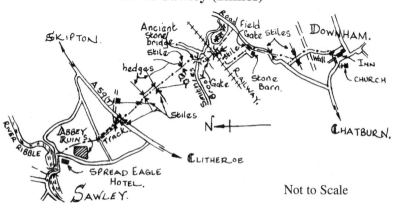

Not to Scale

47

4.4 – Downham to Sawley (2miles)

Access: -
    Downham is accessible by bus from Clitheroe but the major purpose of this link is to connect the main route with the 'Ribble Way' at Sawley.

Route: -
    Leaving Downham along the path opposite the church, which proceeds past a small car park and inn on the right, pass through a wooden gate and turn left alongside a wall to a stile. After climbing the stile, continue along the path bearing slightly right, to a second stile, which gives access to a road just beyond a double bend. Turning right along the road for approximately 100yds, turn left into a gateway just after a stone barn. Proceed down the left hand side of fields towards the railway embankment and then right to a stile giving access to a track, which passes underneath the railway.

    Looking ahead pass through a gate into a field and turn right to reach Smithies Brook, which is crossed by an ancient stone bridge. From the bridge proceed uphill to the left, to a stile beneath a group of trees. Cross the stile and continue diagonally across the field ahead, to a gate and stile leading into the field beyond. Proceed along the right hand hedge of this field to another stile over into the next field, and continue ahead through a gate and across another field to a stile and gate giving access to the A59 trunk road.

    After crossing the A59 trunk road, continue ahead over stiles and along a lane for 300yds, to the junction with another old lane. Proceed through the gateway opposite to cross the field containing the remains of Sawley Abbey on the left and emerge in the village of Sawley opposite the Spread Eagle Hotel.

Points of Interest: -
    The only significant point of interest is the remains of the Cistercian Abbey at Sawley, founded in A.D. 1148.

The Way Ahead: -
    From here there is an infrequent local bus service to Clitheroe and ½mile away along the A59T road, a long distance coach service between Skipton and Preston. Alternatively one may continue to the north or south by 'The Ribble Way', which passes The Spread Eagle Hotel, and to the north joins with 'The Pennine Way' at Horton-in-Ribblesdale.

Link Paths to The Sandstone Trail and Offa's Dyke Path

Apart from forming a direct route from several towns in South Lancashire to 'The Pennine Way', 'The Lancashire Trail' is also a major link between 'The Pennine Way' and 'The Sandstone Trail' in Cheshire which is readily connected to 'The Offa's Dyke' path.

To the south of 'The Lancashire Trail', the local authorities of St. Helens and Warrington have created a linear park along the Sankey Valley, which follows the course of the old St. Helens Canal, and beyond this park the towpath of the canal continues to West Point at Widnes.

On crossing the bridge from Widnes to Runcorn, the towpath of the Bridgewater Canal can be followed to Preston Brook and the towpath of the Trent and Mersey Canal to Dutton Lock. Beyond this lock, a path across fields on the right leads to Dutton Lodge Farm and the lane past this farm continues under the railway to a stile. On passing over this stile and one or two fields, a further lane is reached which proceeds towards the village of Aston. Before reaching this village, a lane on the left, passing Parkside Farm on the right, continues down towards a field across which a path leads to the embankment of the Weaver Navigation Canal.

Turning right along the canal embankment, the path leads to a swing bridge on the A56 trunk road into Frodsham. After ½mile along this road towards Frodsham, a footpath on the left to Overton continues up to the church and onto Frodsham Hill, and the start of 'The Sandstone Trail'.

At the southern end of 'The Sandstone Trail', at Grindley Brook near Whitchurch, the towpath of the Llangollen Canal provides a link to 'The Offa's Dyke' path near Chirk Castle.

In this way, 'The Lancashire Trail' forms a vital link in the country's network of long distance footpaths between South Wales and Scotland or the Yorkshire and Cumbria coasts.

Tourist Information Centres near Route

St. Helens – Information Desk.	Tel. 01744 456951
Wigan – Trencherfield Mill, Wallgate.	Tel. 01942 825677
Rivington Barn.	Tel. 01204 697738
Bolton – Town Hall, Victoria Sq.	Tel. 01204 334400
Blackburn – 15 Railway Road.	Tel. 01254 53277
Burnley – Burnley Mechanics, Manchester Road	Tel. 01282 664421
Clitheroe – High Street.	Tel. 01200 425566
Skipton – 35 Coach Street.	Tel. 01756 792809

Recommended Maps to Accompany this Guide

O.S. Explorer Maps No's: -

275 Liverpool

285 Southport & Chorley

287 West Pennine Moors

OL 21 South Pennines

Grid References of Principal Points on Route

This section has been included to assist all walkers, particularly those who have a G.P.S. system to locate precise positions on route. You may find it helpful to use in conjunction with the relevant O.S. map of the area.

Grid Reference

Start of walk in St. Helens	G.R. 512955
Carr Mill Dam	G.R. 526976
Otters Swift (farm)	G.R. 524988
Main Road, Billinge	G.R. 522995
Billinge Hill, 'trig' point	G.R. 526014
Higher Heaton Farm	G.R. 519026
Roby Mill	G.R. 518072
Ashurst's Beacon	G.R. 501079
Leeds/Liverpool Canal crossing	G.R. 508100
Harrock Hill	G.R. 511132
Toogood Farm	G.R. 525131
Worthington Lakes	G.R. 587110
Little Scotland	G.R. 606107
Anderton Old Hall Farm	G.R. 628117
Rivington Barn	G.R. 633144
Yarrow Reservoir	G.R. 623155
White Coppice	G.R. 623190
M65 Bridge	G.R. 644244
Ravine near Close Farm	G.R. 632277
Arley Brook	G.R. 649293
Mellor Moor 'trig' point	G.R. 657313
Reservoir, Ramsgreave Hall	G.R. 681317
Dean Clough Reservoir	G.R. 716334
Whalley Banks Farm	G.R. 734350
Wiswell Moor Houses	G.R. 757371
Lower Admergill	G.R. 854423
Thornton, Finish	G.R. 907485

High Points on Route

	M	**Feet**
Billinge Beacon	179	582
Ashurst's Beacon	175	569
Harrock Hill	157	510
Little Scotland	141	458
Rivington Barn	180	585
Great Hill	381	1238
Tockholes Plantation	214	695
Wilpshire Moor	205	666
Nick of Pendle	303	985
Black Hill	436	1417
Offa Hill	252	819
Lister Well Road	343	1115
Pendle Hill	563	1831

Distances Between Prominent Points

			Miles	Km
Start	to	Carr Mill Dam	3.2	5.1
Carr Mill Dam	to	Billinge	1.4	2.2
Billinge	to	Up Holland	4.5	7.3
Up Holland	to	Parbold Hill	6.0	9.6
Parbold Hill	to	Coppull Moor	5.5	8.8
Coppull Moor	to	Blackrod	5.25	8.5
Blackrod	to	Rivington Barn	3.0	4.8
Rivington Barn	to	Abbey Village	9.0	14.5
Abbey Village	to	Mellor	8.0	12.9
Mellor	to	Whalley	7.5	12.1
Whalley	to	Barley	7.5	12.1
Barley	to	Thornton in Craven	10.0	16.1
			70.85	114.0

Links

Wigan	to	Arley Hall	4.0	6.4
Bolton	to	Rivington Barn	5.0	8.1
Burnley	to	Barley	6.0	9.6

Approximate Walking Times of Sections

			Hours	**Min.**
Start	to	Carr Mill Dam	1	30
Carr Mill Dam	to	Billinge	0	40
Billinge	to	Up Holland	2	30
Up Holland	to	Parbold Hill	3	30
Parbold Hill	to	Coppull Moor	2	50
Coppull Moor	to	Blackrod	2	40
Blackrod	to	Rivington Barn	1	30
Rivington Barn	to	Abbey Village	4	30
Abbey Village	to	Mellor	4	00
Mellor	to	Whalley	3	45
Whalley	to	Barley	3	45
Barley	to	Thornton in Craven	4	30
			35	40

Links

Wigan	to	Arley Hall	2	00
Bolton	to	Rivington Barn	2	30
Burnley	to	Barley	3	30

The walking times shown above are approximate and will vary depending on fitness, weather conditions, weight of pack and number of walkers in your group. They are given only as a guide and do not include stops.

Public Houses/Hotels on Route

Princess Royal	- -	St. Helens
Ship Inn	- -	Blackbrook
White Lion Hotel	- -	Up Holland
Owl Inn	- -	Up Holland
Abbey Lakes Inn	- -	Up Holland
Fox Inn	- -	Roby Mill
The Wiggin Tree	- -	Parbold Hill
The New Seven Stars Inn	- -	Coppull Moor
The Crown Inn	- -	Worthington
Gallaghers	- -	Little Scotland
Hare & Hounds	- -	Abbey Village
The Boatyard Inn	- -	Riley Green
Clog & Billycock Inn	- -	Near Billinge Hill
The Traders Arms	- -	Mellor
The Pendle Inn	- -	Barley

Useful Addresses

Long Distance Walkers Association (L.D.W.A.)
Brian Smith
10 Temple Park Close
Leeds
L.S.15 0JJ
0113 2642205

This association is set up to further the interests of those who enjoy long distance walking. Members receive a journal three times each year, which includes information on all aspects of long distance walking.

Ramblers Association
2nd Floor
Camelford House
87-90 Albert Embankment
London
SE1 7TW
01577 861222
Local groups which meet regularly.

Hopefully you have enjoyed this walk and gained as much pleasure from walking the route as I did. Should you wish to walk another route, please visit Challenge Publications website at: -

www.chall-pub.co.uk

Here you will find other interesting, and possibly different walks around the British Isles, which are equally as picturesque and enjoyable as this one.
Should you wish to comment on this book or give further information to help keep the book updated then please write to: -

Challenge Publications
7, Earlsmere Drive,
Ardsley
Barnsley
S71 5HH